# HOLLYWORDS

*From Marlon Brando to Mae West
Gems of Wisdom and Outrageous Wit.*

Great Quotations Publishing Company
Glendale Heights, Illinois

Compiled by Michael Ryan
Cover Design by Jeff Maniglia
Typeset and Design by Julie Otlewis

Published in the United Stated by:

Great Quotations Publishing Company,
1967 Quincy Court
Glendale Heights, Illinois 60139


Printed in Hong Kong
ISBN: 1-56245-026-3

Acting is standing up naked
and turning around very slowly.

— Rosalind Russell

I started out to be the sex fiend,
but I couldn't pass the physical.

— Robert Mitchum

There's right and there's wrong.
You got to do one or the other.
You do the one, and your living.
You do the other, and you may be
walking around but you're
dead as a beaver hat.

— John Wayne

I'm not afraid to die.
I just don't want to be there
when it happens.

— Woody Allen

When turkeys mate, they think of swans.

— Johnny Carson

I don't say we all ought to misbehave,
but we ought to look as if we could.

— Orson Welles

If you have never been
hated by your child,
you have never been a parent.

— Bette Davis

I knew I was an unwanted baby
when I saw that my bath toys
were a toaster and a radio.

— Joan Rivers

A painter paints, a musician plays,
a writer writes -
but a movie actor waits.

— Mary Astor

Thank God kids never mean well.

— Lily Tomlin

If you have made mistakes,
even serious ones, there is always
another chance for you.
What we call failure is not
the falling down, but the staying down.

— Mary Pickford

I never met a kid I liked.

— W. C. Fields

Last time I tried to make love to my wife
nothing was happening. So I said to her,
"What's the matter, you can't
think of anybody either?"

— Rodney Dangerfield

Love is the delightful interval between
meeting a beautiful girl and
discovering that she looks like a haddock.

— John Barrymore

I sold my memoirs of my love life
to Parker Brothers and they are going to
make a game out of it.

— Woody Allen

Marriage is a great institution,
but I'm not ready for an institution yet.

— Mae West

Acting is a form of confession.

— Tallulah Bankhead

How do you know love is gone?
If you said that you would be there
at seven and you get there by nine,
and he or she has not called
the police yet - it's gone.

— Marlene Dietrich

If we are not our brother's keeper,
let us at least not be his executioner.

— Marlon Brando

'Twas a woman who drove me to drink,
and I never had the courtesy
to thank her for it.

— W. C. Fields

Inflation has gone up over a dollar a quart.

— W. C. Fields

The less I behave like Whistler's mother
the night before, the more I look like her
the morning after.

— Tallulah Bankhead

If you drink, don't drive. Don't even putt.

— Dean Martin

Ronald Reagan was not a typical politician
because he didn't know how to
lie, cheat, and steal.
He always had an agent for that.

— Bob Hope

Nancy Reagan fell down and broke her hair.

— Johnny Carson

It's not the men in my life that count,
it's the life in my men.

— Mae West

————————  ————————

The really frightening thing about middle age
is the knowledge that you'll grow out of it.

— Doris Day

I don't know the key to success,
but the key to failure is
trying to please everybody.

— Bill Cosby

Success is a public affair.
Failure is a private funeral.

— Rosalind Russell

My passions were all gathered together
like fingers that made a fist.
Drive is considered aggression today;
I knew it then as purpose.

— Bette Davis

I never said , "I want to be alone."
I only said, "I want to be left alone."
There is all the difference.

— Greta Garbo

Divorce is a game played by lawyers.

— Cary Grant

The curtain rises on a vast primitive wasteland,
not unlike certain parts of New Jersey.

— Woody Allen

---

I like a woman with a head on her shoulders.
I hate necks.

— Steve Martin

Love for the joy of loving,
and not for the offerings
of someone else's heart.

— Marlene Dietrich

Husband are like fires.
They go out if unattended.

— Zsa Zsa Gabor, (Miss Hungary, 1936)

Don't ever let me catch you
singing like that again,
without enthusiasm. You're nothing
if you aren't excited by
what you are doing.

— Frank Sinatra to his son, Frank Jr.

California is the only state in the union where you can fall asleep under a rose bush in full bloom and freeze to death.

— W. C. Fields

Many a man owes his success
to his first wife and
his second wife to his success.

— Jim Backus

I never know how much of what I say is true.

— Bette Midler

I'm as pure as the driven slush.

— Tallulah Bankhead

Attempt the impossible
in order to improve your work.

— Bette Davis

If it weren't for Philo T. Farnsworth,
inventor of television,
we'd still be eating frozen radio dinners.

— Johnny Carson

## Do everything.
## One thing may turn out right.

— Humphrey Bogart

Without wonder and insight,
acting is just a trade.
With it, it becomes creation.

— Bette Davis

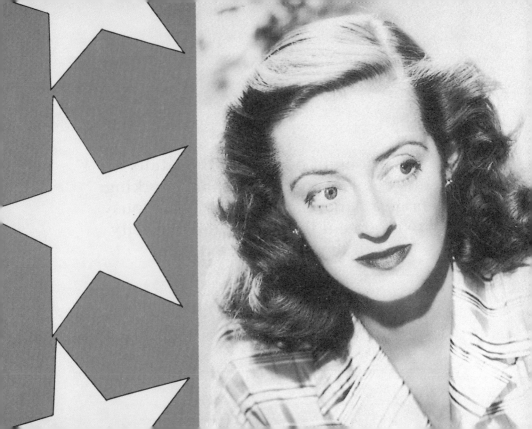

Ninety-eight percent of the adults in
this country are decent, hard-working,
honest Americans. It's the other lousy
two percent that get all the publicity.
But then - we elected them.

— Lily Tomlin

I don't try to guess
what a million people will like.
It's hard enough to know what I like.

— John Huston

I'm astounded by people who want to "know" the universe when it's hard enough to find your way around Chinatown.

— Woody Allen

I talk to myself because I like dealing
with a better class of people.

— Jackie Mason

I only like two kinds of men:
Domestic and foreign.

— Mae West

When I was kidnapped,
my parents snapped into action.
They rented out my room.

— Woody Allen

Integrate what you believe in
every single area of your life.
Take your heart to work and ask the
most and best of everybody else, too.

— Meryl Streep

In a great romance, each person basically plays a part that the other really likes.

— Elizabeth Ashley

I love Mickey Mouse more than
any woman I've ever known.

— Walt Disney

Never say to younger people,
"that was before your time,"
because the last full moon
was before their time.

— Bill Cosby

A man can sleep around, no questions asked,
but if a woman makes nineteen
or twenty mistakes, she's a tramp.

— Joan Rivers

If you want to read about love and marriage
you've got to buy two separate books.

— Alan King

A man in love is incomplete until he is married.
Then he is finished.

— Zsa Zsa Gabor

We all need somebody to talk to.
It would be good if we
talked to each other -
not just pitter-patter, but real talk.
It's so much easier to get along
when we drop our masks.

— Liv Ullmann

What to do when inspiration doesn't come:
Be careful not to spook, get the wind up,
force things into position.
You must wait around until the idea comes.

— John Huston

You have one failing you must overcome,
one thing you must learn if you are
to be a completely happy woman,
maybe the most important lesson in living -
you must learn to say no.
You do not know how to say no, Sophia,
and that is a serious deficiency.

— Charlie Chaplin to Sophia Loren

I don't act, I react.

— Jimmy Stewart

I've been through it all, baby.
I'm Mother Courage.

— Elizabeth Taylor

Whatever you do kid,
always serve it with a little dressing.

— George M. Cohan, to Spencer Tracy

My mother didn't breast-feed me.
She said she liked me as a friend.

— Rodney Dangerfield

If you listen to all the clowns around
you're just dead.
Go do what you have to do.

— James Cagney, advice to John Travolta

Having children is like having a bowling alley
installed in your brain.

— Martin Mull

Smartness runs in my family.
When I went to school I was so smart
my teacher was in my class for five years.

— George Burns

I was thrown out of college for cheating
on the metaphysics exam;
I looked into the soul of the boy next to me.

— Woody Allen

If you don't daydream and kind of plan
the things out in your imagination,
you never get there.
So you have to start someplace.

— Robert Duvall

You do what the script tells you.
Deliver the goods without comment.
Live it - do it - or shut up.
If the script is good and you don't
get in its way, it will come off o.k..

— Katherine Hepburn

I learned you have to trust yourself.
You have got to discover you,
what you do, and trust it.

— Barbara Streisand

Spaghetti can be eaten most successfully if
you inhale it like a vacuum cleaner.

— Sophia Loren

I have to think hard to name
an interesting man who does not drink.

— Richard Burton

Don't stay in bed . . .
unless you can make money in bed.

— George Burns

Stay humble. Always answer your phone -
no matter who else is in the car.

— Jack Lemmon

Somebody left the cork out of my lunch.

— W.C. Fields

The best way to get most husbands
to do something is to suggest that
perhaps they're too old to do it.

— Shirley MacLaine

The only line that's wrong in Shakespeare is
"holding a mirror up to nature."
You hold a magnifying glass up to nature.
As an actor you just enlarge it enough
so that your audience can
identify with a situation.

— Montgomery Clift

Men are creatures with two legs
and eight hands.

— Jayne Mansfield

I was married by a judge.
I should have asked for a jury.

— George Burns

Live your character. It's like skiing,
you can't be thinking too much.
You've got to behave as the character.
A lot of what acting is,
is paying attention.

— Robert Redford

If I had done everything I'm credited with,
I'd be speaking to you from a
laboratory jar at Harvard.

— Frank Sinatra

My old drama coach used to say,
"Don't just do something, stand there."
Gary Cooper wasn't afraid to do nothing.

— Clint Eastwood

For me, life has been either
a wake or wedding.

— Peter O'Toole

One of my chief regrets during my years
in the theater is that I couldn't
sit in the audience and watch me.

— John Barrymore

I always brought up my children not to
believe in Mother's Day gifts,
and now I regret it.

— Lauren Bacall

She's the kind of girl who climbed the ladder of success wrong by wrong.

— Mae West

I was never totally involved in movies.
I was making my father's dream come true.

— Mary Astor

I got started dancing because I knew
that was one way to meet girls.

— Gene Kelly

I did it for the loot, honey,
always for the loot.

— Ava Gardner

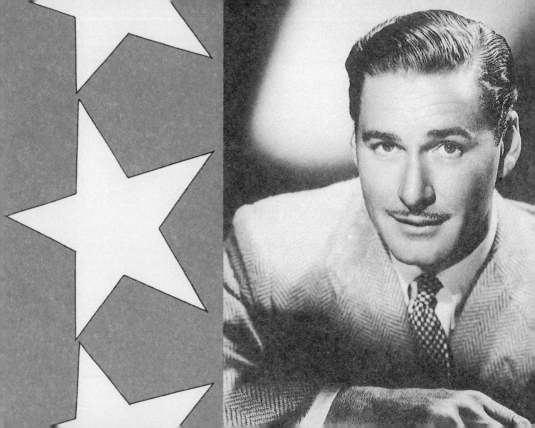

My problem lies in reconciling my
gross habits with my net income.

— Errol Flynn

I've done the most awful rubbish
in order to have somewhere
to go in the morning.

— Richard Burton

I went into business for the money,
and the art grew out of it.
If people are disillusioned by that remark,
I can't help it. It's the truth.

- Charlie Chaplin

It's no longer a question of staying healthy.
It's a question of finding a sickness you like.

— Jackie Mason

I don't deserve this award, but I have arthritis and I don't deserve it either.

— Jack Benny

I'm sick of carrying guns
and beating up women.

— James Cagney

I'm just a hoofer with a spare set of tails.

— Fred Astaire

I made more lousy pictures
than any actor in history.

— Humphrey Bogart

The embarrassing thing is that the
salad dressing is out-grossing my films.

— Paul Newman

I'm exhausted from not talking.

— Sam Goldwyn

## Isn't there any other part of the matzo you can eat?

— Marilyn Monroe on being served matzo ball soup three meals in a row.

No matter how old you get,
if you can keep the desire to be creative,
you're keeping the man-child alive.

— John Cassavetes

I was born at the age of twelve
on the Metro-Goldwyn-Mayer lot.

— Judy Garland

I don't pretend to be an ordinary housewife.

— Elizabeth Taylor

Hollywood - a place where people
from Iowa mistake each other
for movie stars.

— Fred Allen

After age seventy, it's patch, patch, patch.

— Jimmy Stewart

When they said Canada,
I thought it would be up in
the mountains somewhere.

— Marilyn Monroe

Too bad the only people who know
how to run the country are busy
driving cabs and cutting hair.

— George Burns

When we talk to God, we're praying.
When God talks to us we're schizophrenic.

— Lily Tomlin

I have no problem finding girls,
but the world has changed.
Before you take a girl to bed,
you have to discuss the plague.
I can't deal with those sort of negatives
as a form of foreplay.
So I don't bother much.

— Jack Nicholson

I'm still the little southern girl
from the wrong side of the tracks
who really didn't feel like she belonged.

— Faye Dunaway

The last thing I want to be is a
rich black superstar. I just want to act.

— James Earl Jones

Everybody knows that people outside
show business have show business fantasies -
to be an actor, write a script, direct.
What most people don't know is that
people in show business have retail fantasies -
a little restaurant, maybe a ball team.
I want a bookstore.

— Richard Dreyfuss

I came back from the war
and ugly heroes were in.

— Robert Mitchum

Paint eyeballs on my eyelids and
I'll sleepwalk through any picture.

— Robert Mitchum

I always try to balance the
light with the heavy -
a few tears for the human spirit
in with the sequins and the fringes.

— Bette Midler

The public has always expected me
to be a playboy, and a decent chap
never lets his public down.

— Errol Flynn

The only reason I'm in Hollywood is
that I don't have the moral courage
to refuse the money.

— Marlon Brando

Actually, I have no regard for money.
Aside from its purchasing power,
it's completely useless as far as I'm concerned.

— Alfred Hitchcock

I've become a body of films, not a man.
I am all those films.

— Alfred Hitchcock

An associate producer is the only
guy in Hollywood who will
associate with a producer.

— Fred Allen

The dead actor requested in his will
that his body be cremated and
ten percent of his ashes be
thrown in his agents face.

— Unknown

Television has proved that people will look at anything rather than each other.

— Ann Landers

I wish Frank Sinatra would just
shut up and sing.

— Lauren Bacall

I wasn't driven to acting by
an inner compulsion.
I was running away from
the sporting goods business.

— Paul Newman

God makes stars; I just produce them.

— Samuel Goldwyn

If I had my career over again?
Maybe I'd say to myself,
speed it up a little.

— James Stewart

I just got wonderful news from my
real estate agent in Florida.
They found land on my property.

— Milton Berle

I've never looked through a keyhole
without finding someone was looking back.

— Judy Garland

I think one of the deaths of Hollywood
is that producers tried to
make everybody normal.
Nobody would be in this business
if he were normal.

— Vincent Price

If you live to the age of a hundred
you have it made, because very few people
die past the age of a hundred.

— George Burns

When you're on stage, sometimes you
here the best sound a player can hear. . . .
It is the sound of a wonderful,
deep silence that means you've
hit them where they live.

— Shelly Winters

The egg cream is psychologically the
opposite of circumcision -
it pleasurably reaffirms your Jewishness.

— Mel Brooks

The only time a woman really succeeds in changing a man is when he's a baby.

— Natalie Wood

An actress's life is so transitory -
suddenly you're a building.

— Helen Hayes commenting on the news that a
New York theater was being renamed after her.

Whenever I'm caught between two evils,
I take the one I've never tried.

— Mae West

If you become a star, you don't change,
everyone else does.

— Kirk Douglas

To get them to like you,
I figured you sort of had to be their ideal.
I don't mean a handsome knight
riding a white horse, but a fellow who
answered the description of a right guy.

— Gary Cooper

I kept the same suit for six years -
and the same dialogue.
We just changed the title of the picture
and the leading lady.

— Robert Mitchum

_____      _____

The secret of staying young is to live honestly,
eat slowly, and lie about your age.

— Lucille Ball

I smoke cigars because at my age
if I don't have something to hang onto
I might fall down.

— George Burns

I have no regrets.
I wouldn't have lived my life
the way I did if I was going
to worry about what
people were going to say.

— Ingrid Bergman

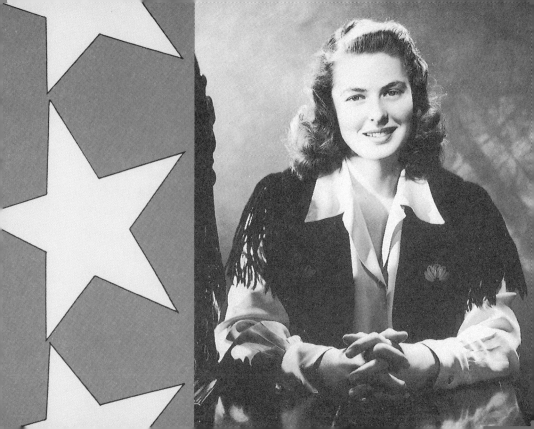

Sometimes I've been to a party
where no one spoke to me
the whole evening. The men were
frightened by their wives or sweeties
and the ladies would gang up in a corner
to discuss my dangerous character.

— Marilyn Monroe

The only thing in acting is the truth;
you have to be truthful to the situation,
whether it's comedy or drama,
whether you're in a three ring circus
or slitting your throat.

— Rex Harrison

Everything you see I owe to spaghetti.

— Sophia Loren

Don't start thinking of yourself
as some kind of la-di-da member
of the elite or you'll
wind up on your ass.

— Spencer Tracy

The way I see it,
if you want the rainbow,
you gotta put up with the rain.

— Dolly Parton

I have an everyday religion
that works for me.
Love yourself first and
everything else falls into line.

— Lucille Ball

I can't play a loser.
I don't look like one.

— Rock Hudson

A verbal contract isn't worth the paper it's written on.

Sam Goldwyn

I'd like to do a love scene
with him just to see what
all the yelling is about.

— Shirley MacLaine (of her brother Warren Beatty)

Elvis Presley had nothing to do with
excellence, just myth.

— Marlon Brando

There are two million interesting people
in New York and only seventy-eight
are in Los Angeles.

— Neil Simon

A bank is a place that will
lend you money if you can prove
that you don't need it.

— Bob Hope

There is nothing wrong with Hollywood that
six first-class funerals wouldn't solve.

— Unknown